DISGUSTING HISTORY

THE ROUGH, STORMY AGE OF VIKINGS

THE DISGUSTING DETAILS ABOUT VIKING LIFE

by James A. Corrick

raintree

a Capstone company — publishers for children

Raintree is an imprint of Capstone Global Library Limited, a company incorporated in England and Wales having its registered office at 264 Banbury Road, Oxford, OX2 7DY – Registered company number: 6695582

www.raintree.co.uk
myorders@raintree.co.uk

Edited by Mari Bolte
Designed by Gene Bentdahl
Picture research by Wanda Winch
Production by Eric Manske

ISBN 978 1 4747 1963 6
19 18 17 16 15
10 9 8 7 6 5 4 3 2 1

British Library Cataloguing in Publication Data
A full catalogue record for this book is available from the British Lib

Photo Credits
akg-images, 19, 27; Alamy Images: Mary Evans Picture Library, 7, N
Archive: Museo Naval Madrid/Gianni Dagli Orti, 15, NGS Image C
N.Y., 21; The Bridgeman Art Library International: Giraudon/Lauros
Art Library International: Nationalmuseum, Stockholm, Sweden/Marten Eskil Winge, 28-29, The Stapleton Collection/Private Collection, 10, The Stapleton Collection/Private Collection/Arthur C. Michael, cover; Capstone: Ross Watton, 5 (bottom left) 14; Corbis: Bettmann, 16-17, Stefano Bianchetti, 9, Ted Spiegel, 22-23; iStockphoto: Andrew Baker, 4 (top left), Duncan Walker, 4 (bottom left), 5 (bottom right), Leif Norman, 11; The Lost Battalion: sculpted by Shane Terry, painted by Mike Butler, 13; Nova Development Corporation, 4 (map), 5 (ships, tombstone); Shutterstock: akva, diary design element, Algol, (right), Denise Kappa, 5 (middle), freelanceartist, grunge design element, Turi Tamas, banner design element; Wikipedia, 24

Primary Source Bibliography
page 13 – from the *Ynglinga Saga* by Snorri Sturluson as published in *The Viking World* by Jacqueline Simpson (New York: St. Martin's Press, 1980).

page 27 – from *Beowulf*, translated by John McNamara (New York: Barnes and Noble, Inc., 2005).

We would like to thank Sherrill Harbison for his invaluable help in the preparation of this book.

Every effort has been made to contact copyright holders of material reproduced in this book. Any omissions will be rectified in subsequent printings if notice is given to the publisher.

Printed and bound in China.

CONTENTS

THE ERA OF THE VIKINGS

AD 793–1066

KEY

VIKING HOMELANDS
VIKING SETTLEMENTS
• • • • ROUTES

0   100 MILES
0   161 KM

N
W ← → E
S

AD 793   PAGE 6

Vikings raid Lindisfarne in England. This is the first recorded Viking attack.

AD 825

Vikings discover Iceland.

PAGE 9   **AD 845**

Vikings raid France and establish Dublin, Ireland.

AD 865

Vikings conquer most of central England.

AD 870

Vikings begin settling Iceland.

AD 911

The Viking leader Rollo becomes Duke of Normandy in France.

VINLAND MAP

In 1965 Yale University in the United States announced that it had a map that proved Vikings had reached North America before Christopher Columbus. Today experts debate whether the "Vinland Map" is real or fake.

PAGE 18   **AD 930**

Vikings in Iceland set up the first European parliament.

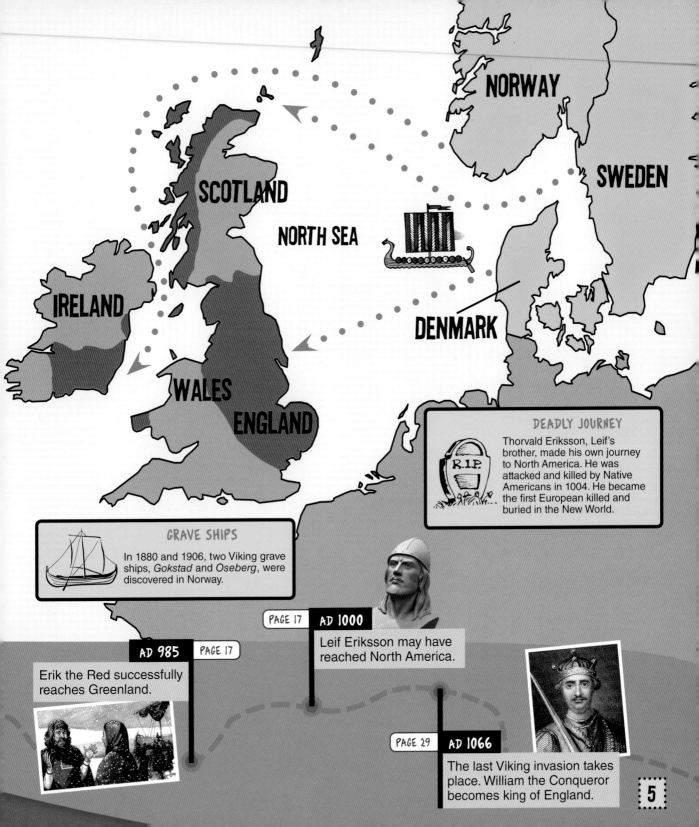

NORWAY

SWEDEN

SCOTLAND

NORTH SEA

IRELAND

DENMARK

WALES

ENGLAND

DEADLY JOURNEY

Thorvald Eriksson, Leif's brother, made his own journey to North America. He was attacked and killed by Native Americans in 1004. He became the first European killed and buried in the New World.

GRAVE SHIPS

In 1880 and 1906, two Viking grave ships, *Gokstad* and *Oseberg*, were discovered in Norway.

PAGE 17 | AD 1000

Leif Eriksson may have reached North America.

AD 985 | PAGE 17

Erik the Red successfully reaches Greenland.

PAGE 29 | AD 1066

The last Viking invasion takes place. William the Conqueror becomes king of England.

RAIDERS FROM THE SEA

For nearly 300 years, a group known as the Vikings terrorized Europe. These men from Scandinavia attacked anywhere their ships could reach. These "Devil Children" were as mean as they were tough.

The first major Viking attack took place in AD 793, at the English holy island known as Lindisfarne. From then on, the Vikings looted towns and villages. They destroyed whole communities. They captured thousands of slaves. Nobody escaped the Vikings.

These wolves of the sea would eventually be tamed by time. But before then, they would come to rule large territories across Europe.

A Viking raid was a fearsome thing. Their ships would appear suddenly and without warning. A single ship could carry about 24 heavily armed warriors. Often there was more than one ship in a raid.

The Vikings were **pagans**. To them, only the strongest and most powerful were meant to rule. The Vikings showed no pity or mercy. They set buildings on fire. They killed men, women and children who tried to escape.

The largest Viking ship ever found could carry 100 warriors.

Vikings took anything of value. Churches were prime targets. They held great treasures, and the monks who lived there did not fight back. The Vikings killed all the animals. It was easier to take animal skins and dried meat with them when they left rather than live animals.

pagan person who is not a member of one of the main world religions

Small raids continued throughout the Viking age.
But over time, the Vikings became more organized. They
built large **fleets** of more than 300 ships. Villagers were
terrified when they saw hundreds of Viking ships sailing
towards their homes.

Vikings needed money to conduct their raids.
They had a number of ways of getting this loot. Sometimes
churches, towns and even whole kingdoms agreed to pay
protection money. The Vikings took the payments and
promised not to attack. It was a good plan. The payments
drained the people of their resources, and the Vikings didn't
have to lift a finger.

Ragnar Lodbrok often attacked on holy days when soldiers would be in church.

In AD 845 an army of Vikings, led by Ragnar Lodbrok, sailed up the River Seine. His fleet of 145 ships attacked Paris, France. The French soldiers were captured and executed. Finally the king of France paid the Vikings' price. He paid nearly 5.4 tonnes of silver and gold. Paying the ransom was a mistake. Other Viking groups heard of the rich bribe and came to claim their own.

Vikings also fought among themselves. Vikings from Denmark and Norway fought over land in Ireland. The Viking settlement of Dublin changed hands several times.

fleet group of ships

The history of the Vikings has been recorded in stories since around the 13th century AD.

FOUL FACT

One group of Vikings celebrated war victories by having a feast on the battlefield. They set up their cooking fires among the bodies. The fire cooked their food and burned the bodies of their enemies.

ROUGH AND TOUGH BATTLES

What's more scary – knives, swords or battle-axes? The victims of the Vikings' raids were faced with answering that question. Villagers were often unarmed. The Vikings could easily cut down these defenceless people.

In war, Vikings usually found themselves facing a well-armed enemy. Wounds could be nasty, and sometimes proved fatal. Iron swords sliced at bodies, arms and legs. Sometimes limbs were cut off. A strong blow from a sword or axe could split a person's head open. A thrown battle-axe could lodge itself in a body.

Vikings wore armour that covered their chests and backs. Most armour was made of toughened leather, which offered protection without a lot of weight. Some Vikings wore chain mail made of linked metal rings. Others wore steel or leather helmets on their heads. Arms and legs were left bare so they could move more easily. Most Viking warriors carried a round wooden shield.

CHAIN MAIL

Warriors called berserkers were especially feared. Some Viking leaders kept these warriors in their armies. The berserkers fought without fear of death. They worked themselves into a wild frenzy called a Berserk Rage. Their only desire during this rage was to kill.

Berserkers did not wear armour or helmets. Instead, they covered their bodies in animal skins. Berserkers were hard to stop even when badly or fatally wounded. In their fury, it was said that they didn't feel any pain.

The existence of berserkers was first recorded in the 9th century AD.

Berserkers

They advanced without mail-coats, and were as frenzied as dogs or wolves; they bit their shields; they were as strong as bears or boars; they struck men down, but neither fire nor steel could mark them. This was called the Berserk Rage.

From a history of the kings of Norway, written by Icelandic historian Snorri Sturluson.

FIERCE ADVENTURES

Vikings did more than raid and loot. They also traded in foreign lands. They explored the Atlantic Ocean. And they settled distant shores. Above all, Vikings sought adventure.

Viking ships were **vessels** for adventure. Their wooden boats, called longships, were engineering marvels. They could be powered by sail or by oar. They were fast, sturdy and easy to steer. And their design made it possible to sail in as little as 50 centimetres (20 inches) of water. This ability allowed Vikings to travel across oceans and up rivers. They could easily sail to distant towns and cities and attack.

Vessels sailing across the ocean were fitted with a dragon or serpent head. The head was to frighten away evil spirits and sea monsters. These heads earned Viking boats the name "Dragon Ships".

All Viking ships were made of wood. Oak was used to build warships.

Viking ships leaked and were often in danger of sinking. Sometimes they did sink. Crews had to spend long hours bailing out water.

Viking ships had no cabins. There was no protection from the weather. Crews were often wet from seawater thrown by wind and waves. Constantly being hit with seawater was hard on the skin. The irritated skin would break out in sores. The salty water stung and kept the sores from healing.

vessel boat or ship

Viking cargo ships, called knorrs, were higher and wider than longships. They also had cargo decks to store supplies. Knorrs could be crowded and smelly places. Settlers travelling to Viking settlements brought their farm animals aboard. Animal waste covered the ship. There was nowhere to go to escape the smell. There was also no privacy when a passenger had to go to the toilet.

A Viking trading ship.

The food could be as rough as the seas. Nothing was cooked, as the risk of starting a fire on a wooden ship was too great. Tough dried meat was washed down with lukewarm water, ale or sour milk.

The ships may have been dangerous and uncomfortable, but they were the most advanced and seaworthy ships of their time. They carried Vikings on many adventures. They allowed Vikings to cross the North Atlantic. Vikings settled in Ireland and Greenland. And eventually they reached North America.

VIKING HOMES

Vikings were more than sailors or raiders. Even though they spent so much time at sea, they had to call somewhere home. They had families. They raised animals and grew their own food. They were also members of society.

Viking societies were ruled differently, depending on where they were. In some societies, the king was in charge. Vikings in Iceland were ruled by a **parliament**. They did not have a king until 1265.

Below the ruling class were **aristocrats**. These were **chieftains** and important landowners. Most Vikings were free commoners. At the bottom of society were the slaves. The slaves were people taken captive during raids. Slave men and women were given the hardest, most gruelling jobs. They had no rights and were seen as property.

Viking towns were built near the sea. The houses were close together for protection against enemies.

parliament group of people who make laws
aristocrat member of the highest rank or nobility
chieftain leader of a group of people

There were some Viking trading towns. But most Vikings lived in one-room houses on farms. The family, farm tenants and slaves all slept together in the house. Benches along the wall served as beds. There was no privacy.

The winters in much of the Vikings' world were long and hard. A Viking farmhouse had thick walls made of wood, stone or dirt. There were no windows. A hole in the roof let out some of the smoke from cooking fires. But the house was dark, smoky and smelly.

The roofs of Viking houses were built to look like their ships.

This is what the inside of a Viking home may have looked like.

Animals had to be kept indoors when it got dark. Otherwise they might freeze to death during cold winter nights. Large farms had barns for the animals. But for many, the house was the only place to put the animals.

The animals provided warmth in the cold winter. But there was a downside. Farm animals aren't house-trained. Straw was laid out to soak up manure and was removed regularly. Still, with no windows to let in fresh air, the smell of soiled straw remained.

The animals could go to the toilet inside, but that didn't work for people. Viking houses did not have toilets. People used open pits dug in the ground outside the house. In the hotter months, these pits would fill the air with their foul stench. Swarms of flies would buzz around anyone who came near.

ROTTEN FOOD AND BROKEN BONES

Most Viking families farmed much of the food they ate. Barley became bread and porridge. Meat came from pigs, horses, cows, goats and chickens. The Vikings used every part of the animal. Blood sausage was a favourite dish. Cows and goats produced milk. There were also beans, cabbage and other vegetables. And Vikings caught fish.

Cold winters prevented Vikings from growing food all year round. In some northern areas, the growing period was very short. Methods of food preservation included pickling, smoking, drying and salting.

Vikings used a process called **fermentation** to preserve some foods. Fermentation prevents bacteria from growing on food. It allows the food to last longer. Today we use fermentation to make vinegar or alcohol.

But the Vikings did more than make vinegar. They would bury an entire animal in a pit and leave it until it soured. Shark meat, whale meat and blubber, fish and butter were just some of the items left in the ground to eat later.

But by the end of a long winter, food was in short supply. People were sometimes half-starved by the time winter ended. They also suffered from illnesses such as **scurvy**.

Vikings ate two meals every day, at sunrise and sunset.

fermentation food preservation technique

scurvy deadly disease caused by a lack of vitamin C

Men who fought after being wounded were seen as the bravest warriors.

Vikings faced other health threats. Even a powerful, berserker Viking couldn't defeat lice or fleas. No amount of sword swinging or axe throwing could give the Vikings a victory. They bathed once a week, but there was no getting rid of these bugs. Some pests lived inside the body. Tapeworms were common. These creatures made their homes in the small intestine. They can grow to be 30 centimetres (1 foot) long. Tapeworms also caused disease, infection and even brain damage.

Vikings did not have doctors. Women were the only healers. They used various plants for medicines. They set broken bones.

Viking women also treated battle wounds. To stop bleeding, they rolled hot iron over the wound. This painful process also prevented infection.

Swords and spears were dangerous and deadly. They could easily pierce a man's body. A warrior with a pierced gut would almost certainly die. The women fed some wounded Vikings a porridge made with onions. If an onion smell came from the wound, then everyone knew the gut had been broken open.

BLOODY JUSTICE

Vikings did not have written laws. Few people could read or write. They also had no police or prisons. But they did have laws. Justice was left in the hands of those who had been wronged.

Most guilty people had to pay a fine to the injured party. Sometimes the convicted person was outlawed. Both fines and outlawing were common punishments for murder.

Someone found guilty of stealing, evil sorcery or lying faced death. Hanging was the most common punishment. But Vikings also cut off heads or burned people alive.

Some Vikings had a system of justice called a blood feud. A person who believed himself wronged by another did not always seek justice. Instead, he or his relatives would kill a member of the wrongdoer's family. This killing often sparked a series of revenge killings between the two families. These feuds could last for generations.

FOUL FACT

Slaves guilty of murder faced a harsh death. Their hands and feet were cut off. Then they were left to die slowly of starvation, blood loss and lack of water.

No home, no honour

Deserting during battle was seen as a horrible crime.
The character Wiglaf in the poem "Beowulf" strips deserters
of their property and honour.

Every one of your kindred will be made to move on, with the
rights to his land stripped away, when war-chieftains from afar hear
the tale told of your flight from your lord, that deed without glory.
Death is better for all noble men, than a life of shame!

GODS OF VIOLENCE

The Vikings believed in many gods. Each god represented a different aspect of life, including war or strength. The chief god was one-eyed Odin. He was often shown riding his eight-legged horse, along with two ravens and two wolves. The goddess Frigg, who represented love and marriage, was Odin's wife. Another important god was Thor. Thor was the god of thunder and lightning. He had a hammer that would always return to him.

Vikings believed giants were the enemies of the gods. The god Loki fought on both sides. Loki had half-giant children. One child was a large snake called the Midgard Serpent. Another was a huge wolf called Fenrir.

Vikings offered the gods both human and animal **sacrifices**. One group hanged nine of every type of male creature, including men, as a gift to the gods every nine years. Another group sacrificed 99 people and 99 horses. They also killed a large number of dogs and cockerels.

Sacrifices were not limited to the gods. Slaves, horses and dogs of an important Viking sometimes joined their master in death too.

The Viking age came to an end in England with the rule of William the Conqueror. By this time, other countries had strong leaders who lived in big castles and had large armies. It became harder and harder for the Vikings to go on successful raids. The Viking way of life died out.

Thor was a well-loved Viking god.

sacrifice kill an animal or person in order to honour a god

GLOSSARY

aristocrat member of the highest social rank or nobility

chieftain leader of a group of people

fermentation food preservation technique that prevents organisms from growing

fleet group of ships

pagan person who is not a member of one of the main world religions

parliament group of people who make law

sacrifice kill an animal or person in order to honour a god

scurvy deadly disease caused by a lack of vitamin C; scurvy produces swollen limbs, bleeding gums and weakness

vessel boat or ship

READ MORE

Norse Myths and Legends (All About Myths), Anita Ganeri (Raintree, 2013)

The Vikings and Anglo-Saxons: The Struggle for the Kingdom of England (Early British History) Claire Throp (Raintree, 2015)

Vikings, Stephanie Turnbull (Usborne, 2015)

Vikings (Explore!), Jane Bingham (Wayland, 2015)

WEBSITES

www.bbc.co.uk/schools/primaryhistory/vikings
Learn about Viking settlements, trade and more.

www.dkfindout.com/uk/history/vikings
Discover facts about life as a Viking.

INDEX